Color Nature Library

BABY ANIMALS

By
JANE BURTON

Designed by
DAVID GIBBON

Produced by
TED SMART

CLB
PUBLISHING

INTRODUCTION

Baby animals appeal to us all. We are delighted by their soft fur, their chubbiness, their uncoordinated movements, and their look of wide-eyed innocence. We tend to like animals that mimic ourselves, such as bears, owls and penguins that walk upright, or parrots and mynah birds that talk. We also like baby animals that show the attributes of our own babies, having a short face with high rounded forehead, bulgy cheeks and large forward-looking eyes. For this reason we particularly fall for kittens, spaniel puppies and baby owls.

The undoubted appeal to us of baby animals that do not look much like human babies is harder to explain. Foals, calves and lambs have sideways-looking eyes, but the eyes are large and such babies do have a short muzzle and rounded head, and small ears, another baby feature. Their legs are outsize, and their movements uncoordinated; maybe this is their greatest appeal to us.

Perhaps the babies which ought most to appeal to us are those of animals closest to ourselves on the family tree, the monkeys and apes. Just as adult gorillas and chimpanzees often look almost too human for our peace of mind, so their babies closely resemble our own babies. A new-born monkey is not quite so helpless as a human baby. It obviously appeals very strongly to all the adult monkeys in its family circle, partly because of its tiny size, its little clinging pink hands, its wrinkly pink face and its quaint movements. Its colour also has a very strong emotional appeal. Many baby monkeys are a different colour from their parents; they have black hair which contrasts with the pinkness of their face, hands and feet. As the baby grows, its skin darkens and its fur lightens to the adult colour, and consequently the baby gradually loses its appeal to its mother. This allows the mother to wean the child and frees the child so that it can live an unattached life playing with other youngsters. However, its size and behaviour still appeal to the adult males in its troop, who continue to feel fiercely protective towards it and tolerate its cheekiness towards them.

Animal babies that have perhaps a little less appeal to us are those that are born at a very early stage of development, such as those of kangaroos and mice. There is a certain charm in such clean new little creatures with their rounded muzzles, sucking mouths and delicate tiny claws. And they ought to appeal to us because their soft hairless pink skin makes them look like miniatures of our own babies. Perhaps because they are blind at birth we do not coo over them so much, and yet we love our own babies when their eyes are peacefully closed in sleep.

It is perhaps a very obvious thing that every animal baby appeals most to the species which gave it birth. If this were not so, mother animals would not care so meticulously for their own babies, or rush to their defence so courageously. In part a mother's response to her babies is an instinctive reaction to shape or smell or colour, but especially to the cries it makes. Every human mother knows the powerful effect the crying of her own baby has; an infant only has to utter one squawk in the night and its mother will be instantly wide awake, needing to go to it. The cries of baby animals have a similar effect on their mothers: the gerbil, hearing high-pitched peepings from her nestlings will rush to warm and feed them, or remove them from danger; the baboon allowing other females to hold her new baby, will insist on having it back if it so much as whimpers.

In most animals the survival of the young depends on the close bond between a mother and her offspring. Nestling babies play a passive part in establishing and maintaining the parent-young bond. But in babies born at a more advanced stage, such as foals, lambs, calves and other hoofed young, the babies play an active part. Young that can walk or swim soon after birth, must follow the mother from the birthplace. So it is crucial that they quickly recognise the right object as their mother and become emotionally attached to it, otherwise they may follow the wrong animal or try to suck from the corner of a tree trunk. These babies are not born with the instinct to recognise their own mother, but must develop that power rapidly in order to survive. They therefore become attached to the first object they see after birth, and fortunately in most cases this is their own mother. This is known as imprinting, and is the means of ensuring the survival of the baby. The mother, as quickly, learns the smell, shape and cries of her own infant, so the two-way bond is firmly established during the first minutes of a baby animal's life.

In this book we are looking only at baby mammals–that is, 'animals' in the traditional sense, not in the zoological sense as meaning the whole of the animal kingdom. All mammal mothers feed their babies at first on milk secreted by their own bodies, and it is this that sets them apart from all other animals.

Previous page, Grey Squirrel.
Left, Roe Deer.

Big Cat Cubs

Lion cubs *top left* are entirely charming; tubby, affectionate, and mischievous, but with the same expressive amber eyes as their parents. There are usually three to four in a litter, but may be as many as six or as few as one. The lion takes no part in caring for his offspring, but the mother very often shares the responsibility with another lioness, often her own sister who may also have young cubs. Together the two females care for all the cubs, suckling them indiscriminately and taking turns with the guarding while the other goes off hunting.

A Tiger cub *bottom left* is another irresistible charmer. As with lions there are usually one to six tiger cubs in a litter, which the tigress hides away in a secret lair. They are weaned at about six weeks, but remain dependant on their mother for another two years.

Cheetah cubs, like lion and tiger cubs, are born blind; their eyes open in about a week. At first cheetah cubs have a mane of long silvery-grey hair extending down the back, but at ten weeks most of this cape is lost. The mother cheetah *right* cares for the cubs on her own.

Tabby Kittens

There are many kinds of small wild cats living in various parts of the world. Many are tabbies and look much like domestic tabby cats. It is difficult to be sure which species of wild tabby was the ancestor of the domestic cat, but the African Wild Cat is the most likely. The tabby pattern is the characteristic of the wild ancestor least changed by domestication, for though domestic kittens come in a wide range of colours–black, white, grey, ginger, tortoiseshell, blue, chocolate and Siamese–the most common colour is still tabby *bottom right*.

A Siamese mother cat or queen will produce Siamese kittens when mated with a male Siamese. But the factor that produces this distinctive coloration is recessive, so that if she mates with a non-Siamese tom, her litter may contain kittens of any colour, even plebeian tabby *top left*. First generation Siamese crosses retain the Siamese shape and voice, and the Siamese wickedness of the kittens, and grow into really beautiful cats, whether tabby, tortoiseshell or black.

The aristocratic appearance of Siamese kittens *top right* belies their tabby forebears. When new-born, Siamese kittens are white, but as they grow their dark points begin to show. Their unusual coloration is the result of a hereditary factor which determines that the fur on the warmer parts of the body stays pale, while the fur on the cooler extremities is dark. Sleepy Siamese kittens look like little angels, but they are wickedness on four paws when awake.

The Bobcat *bottom left* is the wildcat of America. Kits are usually born in early spring, in a den such as a hollow log or cave. There are usually two young in a litter. The mother defends them fiercely, and keeps the father away until the kits are weaned, when she may allow him to help her collect food for them. Like all wild cat kittens, baby bobcats are little spitfires beneath the soft fur, not easily tamed even when taken very young and hand-reared. Domestic kittens, on the other hand, readily accept human company, so domestication must have meant undergoing profound psychological changes before the wildcat ancestor became the tame domestic puss.

Even the thoroughly domesticated and pedigreed cat has departed less from its wild ancestors than has that other intimate household pet, the dog. Cats are nocturnal hunters, and it is at night that purring puss, so docile and contented by day, goes on the prowl and becomes the untamed carnivore. When hunting, cats are silent and solitary; but occasionally they will gather round, crouched on walls and beneath bedroom windows, and produce loud and discordant vocalizations. Such serenading is usually the voices of the males, or toms, disputing territorial rights or seeking to impress a female. Females come on heat at intervals of three to nine days if not mated. Gestation usually lasts just over two months. There may be eight kittens in a litter, but very young or old queens may produce only one or two, while a litter of thirteen has been recorded. The kittens are born blind and deaf, but their eyes open in a few days. They are weaned at about two months, but often stay with the mother and get an occasional suck until quite a lot older.

The Large-spotted Genet *centre* is not a true cat but belongs to the mongoose family; it looks like a cross between a tabby cat and a mongoose. There are several species of genet; all are lightly-built, agile climbers that live mostly in Africa. Females may produce two litters a year, of two or three kits in each.

More Cubs and a Puppy

Brown bear females give birth to their two or three cubs while hibernating in their winter dens. They rouse from their slumbers to bite through the umbilical cords and lick the cubs dry. Then they go back to sleep for another two months, while the cubs alternately suck and sleep. When the mother bear wakes and emerges in the spring the cubs are well furred. They will stay with her until at least a year old *top left*.

The Kodiak Bear *top right* is the largest and the most powerful living carnivore. An adult standing upright is nearly twice as tall as a man. Yet babies are tiny at birth—no larger than a rat—blind, toothless and naked.

The Grizzly Bear *bottom right*, though not as huge as the Kodiak, is a powerful killer, yet a Grizzly cub seems to us a most endearing little creature.

Its very domed head and floppy ears give the Cocker Spaniel puppy its special appeal *centre*.

A Red Fox cub *bottom left* is also a charming baby, with its soft brown fur, short muzzle and innocent expression.

Great Ape Babies

Chimpanzees *left* live in the tropical rain forests of Africa, in small family parties of one or more females and young with attendant males. An older mother chimp may have several children with her. Twins are rare, more usually a single baby is born. Chimpanzee mothers vary as much as human mothers in the care of their young; some babies are over-cossetted, others a bit neglected, but mostly they are neither spoilt nor bullied. For two years a baby is completely dependant on its mother and will be carried everywhere. Gradually it experiments with climbing off its mother and clambering among branches, adventuring away for longer periods to play with other youngsters, and even with the tolerant adult males. By the time a young chimp is four years old its mother may well have another baby, so the elder child has to fend more for itself.

The Orang-utan *top right* is less closely related to man than is the gorilla or chimpanzee, and is found only in Borneo and Sumatra. Strictly an animal of tropical forests–its name means 'Man of the woods' in Malay–it rarely comes to the ground, but spends its life swinging about the trees. Unlike its cousins, orangs do not form large social groups: adult males live alone most of the time, but females with babies sometimes form small nursery groups. A baby clings tight to its mother's fur at first, and later follows her, clinging to her rump hair. At about 5 years old orangs leave their mothers and join up into adolescent gangs.

The Gorilla *bottom right* is the largest of the man-like apes. An adult male may stand as tall as a man, but though immensely powerful and strong he is a gentle, peaceful creature, entirely vegetarian, and an exemplary father. In the wild, gorillas live in small family troops in the forests of Central Africa. The females give birth at any season of the year, after a gestation period slightly shorter than our own. Their babies weigh less than human babies at birth, but they develop twice as fast: their eyes can focus after only one or two weeks, they crawl at nine weeks, walk a few steps at nine months. They become jet black a few days after birth, unlike baby chimps that only darken as they grow up. Infants in a troop have great games together, and also romp over their father who tolerates much cheek from them. Young females become mature at 6 or 7 years old, males at 12 or 14.

13

Suckling

All female mammals produce milk in their bodies to nourish their new-born babies. All new-born mammals have a strong instinct to search for the milk. A baby ungulate, such as a Wildebeest, must find part of its mother's body that makes a corner, where a leg joins the body. Usually it quickly finds the right corner, where it nuzzles until it contacts a teat. Occasionally a calf finds the wrong corner and searches between the front legs *middle left*. The mother does nothing to help her baby, but eventually it finds the correct corner and gets its first suck *bottom left*.

Mammals that give birth to large litters of babies are supplied with a comparable number of teats. Domestic pigs have 8-12 teats; the mother helpfully lies on her side so that her piglets can feed conveniently in two tiers *top left*.

The first flow of milk is called the colostrum, and is very important to the baby. It contains proteins which pass directly into the baby's bloodstream through the stomach wall, giving instant nourishment at the first suck. It also contains some of the mother's antibodies which give the baby immunity to diseases to which the mother has built up a resistance. The immunity lasts all the while the baby is taking milk, but at weaning it faces a dangerous period when it may no longer be immune. The weaning process is a gradual one, however, allowing the young animal to build up its own resistance. This pony foal *top centre*, although still taking some milk, also grazes the summer grasses of the New Forest for itself.

As in all monkeys the Vervet's teats are located between the front legs *top right*. This is an adaptation to an arboreal life; the baby clings beneath its mother's tummy and suckles as she climbs. When the mother is progressing on all fours, it doesn't matter to a baby which end of her the teats are. But when the mother sits on her haunches, which she does frequently, it would be very inconvenient for the baby to be trying to feed upside down if the teats were where they are in many other kinds of mammals, between the hind legs.

On the other hand an elephant's teats actually are located in a front corner. Adult elephants drink by sucking up water in the trunk and squirting it down the throat, but a baby African Elephant sucks direct with its mouth like any other baby *bottom right*.

15

Nests

The babies of many small mammals are born naked, blind and helpless. To keep them safe and warm during the first few weeks of life, the mother makes a nest out of dry grass or leaves, lined with finely-shredded material. The Edible Dormouse *left* makes, her nest in a hollow tree. Baby Common Shrews *top right* are born in a nest of leaves hidden under a fallen log or among tree roots. The doe European Rabbit digs a special underground nursery burrow called a stop. A few days before her young are due she makes a nest of grass lined with fur pulled from her own breast in which the babies will be warm and safe *bottom right*, until their eyes and ears are open, their bodies well-furred and they are old enough to start venturing out to feed themselves.

Babies in Pouches

The Kangaroo *left* is a marsupial or pouched mammal found only in Australia. As with all marsupials its young are born at a very early stage of development, more immature even than nest babies. A kangeroo mother as tall as a man gives birth to a tiny, embryo-like, bean-sized baby. A few minutes before giving birth the female licks her pouch clean and also licks a path from birth canal to pouch. The baby emerges head first and makes its own way by clawing with its front legs up the damp fur and into its mother's pouch. There it fastens onto a teat to feed and grow for 8 months. When old enough the young kangaroo joey sticks its head out of the pouch to watch the outside world. The Swamp Wallaby *top right* has a similar life history. In time the joeys emerge for short trial hops, but return to the pouch to sleep or be carried away from danger. The young Koala *bottom right*, when too large for the pouch, rides pick-a-back on its mother.

Active Babies

A Kangaroo baby is retained within its mother's body for about 33 days, baby mice for up to 21 days; baby rabbits for 30-40 days. This period within the mother's body–the gestation period– is prolonged in some small mammals so that the young are born at a much more advanced state of development, fully-furred, with eyes open, and able to scamper about very soon after birth. Such precocial babies do not need a very well-hidden or warm nest, nor do they need to be carried about in pouches by their mothers. They start to experiment with solid food when only a day or two old and are soon weaned and independent.

Brown Hare leverets *top left* may be born at almost any time of the year. There are usually two to four in a litter. At first they stay bunched together in a form made by the mother, well-camouflaged by their speckled brown fur. Soon they disperse each to its own form where the mother visits them to suckle. By a month old they are independent of her.

Guinea Pigs *bottom left* have a gestation of up to 71 days, exceptionally long for such a small mammal. There may be one to six in a litter; up to 12 have been recorded, but four is a more usual and comfortable number. The mother has only one pair of nipples, yet can raise more than that number of babies because they start to feed themselves within a day or two. They are weaned by 21 days.

The Arabian Spiny Mouse *top right* is unique among mouse-like Old World rodents in giving birth to precocial young. The female has a gestation time twice as long as that of other kinds of mice. The two or three babies are born fully furred and active but not spiny. Adult spiny mice are not as prickly as hedgehogs, but their spines are probably enough to deter snakes from making a meal of them.

The Coypu *bottom right*, a South American rodent, looks like a rat but belongs to the porcupine family among which precocial young are the rule. The aquatic coypu has a gestation of 100-132 days; its young are well-furred and able to swim when only hours old. The mother has teats on her sides so can suckle her babies while swimming.

Water Babies

Babies of truly aquatic mammals such as whales are born at sea; the mother cannot come ashore, so must give birth in the water, lifting the baby to the surface for its first breath. But the young of amphibious mammals such as the Grey Seal *top left* are born on land. The cows come ashore at a definite breeding season to give birth to their pups on traditional breeding beaches. For three weeks the pups are suckled on rich milk; they grow fast and put on a good layer of blubber. After the three weeks the cows return to the sea, abandoning the weanling pups. These now moult out of their white baby coats and spend the next few weeks living on their blubber while they splash about in rock pools learning to swim and fend for themselves.

Unlike the seals that stay with their young for only three weeks, Sea Lion cows do not desert their pups but return every day to suckle them for up to a year *top right*. Sea Lion pups can swim at an early age, and the mothers help them if they get into difficulties at sea.

The very rare Southern Right Whale *centre right* is a peaceful creature hunted from its former abundance almost to extinction by whalers. Although now fully protected by law it is slow in recovering its numbers because females give birth to a single calf only every three years. A Right Whale mother is extraordinarily tolerant of her boisterrous baby, whom she allows to play all over her for hours as she rests. It butts her sides, slides on and off her back, and generally has high jinks all over her.

Occasionally a Hippopotamus birth may take place in the water, but normally the mother prepares a bed of trampled reeds on land. Within minutes the new-born baby hippo can walk and swim *bottom left*. Hippo mothers congregate with others that have babies of the same age, so the youngsters have plenty of playmates to romp with in the water.

Common or Harbour Seal pups are born on sandbanks or rocks between one high tide and another. They shed their baby coats either before or immediately after birth, and are able to swim as soon as the tide comes in. For the first few days the pup floats near shore, closely attended by its mother *bottom right*.

Herd Babies

Babies born into a herd derive safety from numbers. In some species all the mothers give birth to their single calves almost simultaneously, producing so many babies at once that predators such as jackals and hyenas can only take a few during the glut. The remaining babies therefore have a greater chance of survival than if the births had been spread out. Most infant antelopes such as Springbok *top left* move off with the herd as soon as they can walk. Once able to run they rely on speed to out-distance predators. Bison calves *bottom left*, on the other hand, are actively defended by the powerful adult bulls and cows of the herd, which cluster round to protect them from their main enemy the wolf. Giraffes *right* too defend their offspring, by kicking out with flailing hoofs as the baby takes shelter under its mother's belly. Giraffes sometimes leave their young in a crèche with another baby-sitting female who may oversee up to a dozen calves; with her watch-tower view she can see from a long way off if danger threatens.

Horse Babies

In the wild, foals are generally born into small herds consisting of mares and their young led by a stallion. He defends his family by kicking out with his hind feet, even biting savagely.

The ass is a member of the horse family. Only a few truly wild asses are left today, but half-wild donkeys roam some deserts *top left*. Descendants of wild asses, they are true desert animals and can survive on very poor grazing. The nursing mare gets much of the moisture she needs from dew and grass stems, with occasional drinks from a water-hole.

Zebras are no more nor less than wild horses with striped coats, and they behave much as other wild horses. A very young Common Zebra foal *bottom right* has a shaggy coat and brown stripes; it is short in the body and long in the leg like any other young foal.

In Britain ponies have roamed free for centuries, giving rise to distinctive regional breeds. One of the prettiest of these is the Welsh pony *bottom left*.

All members of the horse family are able to interbreed, but their young are sterile and cannot themselves breed. The most familiar cross is the mule, offspring of a horse mother and a donkey father. This is an exceedingly sturdy ass-like animal, whereas the hinny, offspring of a donkey mother and horse father, is horse-like, smaller and less sturdy. Zebra crosses have been obtained with horses and donkeys; this Zeedonk foal with its donkey mother *top right* had a zebra father.

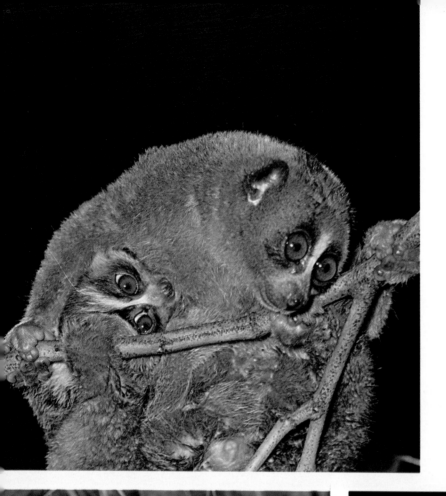

Single Babies

The Slow Loris *top left* is a distant relative of the monkeys and lives in the jungles of south-east Asia. She gives birth to one infant at a time as part of her adaptation to an arboreal life; she could not easily move through the branches if she had to carry more than one baby clinging to her fur. Most hoofed mammals also have a single baby at a birth. To produce more than one large infant at a time would impose an unnecessary burden on the mother, who must remain fleet of foot in order to preserve herself and her unborn infant alive. Not all ungulates live in herds; a small antelope such as the Steinbuck hides her fawn away in long grass, leaving it in seclusion *bottom left*, visiting only to suckle it. But the baby Black Rhinoceros *right* keeps very close to its mother, who defends it with great tenacity if danger threatens. Bats too give birth to single young, for females could easily become too heavy to fly if they had to carry more than one baby. At first a new-born bat clings to its mother's fur but later is left at home in the nursery roost—a huge limestone cavern for this baby Malayan Leaf-nosed Bat *bottom centre*.

Twins

Although single babies are most usual among hoofed mammals, twins do occasionally occur, more especially among deer and goats, much more rarely among antelopes, horses and cattle. Among domestic goats twins are quite usual *left*; exceptionally a nanny may produce three or four kids at a birth. Moose, the largest living deer, are said to have a single calf the first time they breed, but give birth to twins thereafter *top right* and even triplets occasionally. Brown Bears have rather small families by carnivore standards; they normally have twins, sometimes triplets. The cubs remain with their mother for at least a year, learning to find berries and wild honey, and to catch salmon in the river *bottom right*.

31

Animal Families

The human ideal of a happy family unit is of mother and father sharing in the care of their offspring. Among animals this is the exception rather than the rule. More usually it is the mother alone who feeds and protects the babies, even actively driving their father away from them. Single-parent families are common among small mammals such as the European Hedgehog *top left* who is by nature a solitary animal. Babies are born with a few blunt bendy prickles, but by the time they leave the nest they are well covered with stiff, sharp little prickles. By this time their mother is probably expecting her next litter, so if the youngsters do not take themselves off, she will drive them away by butting their sides and rolling them along, snorting fiercely as she does so.

The Golden Hamster *bottom left* is also a solitary little beast. Male and female come together only briefly for mating, then continue on their separate ways. When the young are born the female drives all other hamsters away from the vicinity of the nest, as there is a real danger of the young being killed and eaten by another adult. Young hamsters stay with their mother until about half grown, when they are ready to fend for themselves.

Among many of the hoofed animals such as horses, cattle, elephants, some antelopes and some of the larger deer, the family unit may be a herd of females with young of various ages, guarded by one male in his prime. Among some of the smaller antelopes and deer, such as the Muntjac *top right*, the family may consist of a buck and one or two does with their single or twin fawns. They may not stay close together all the time, but keep in touch by smell and sight if they wander apart while feeding.

Many monkeys and their relatives live in family troops. In a Ring-tailed Lemur troop there may be more males than females. The males have a strict social order, but all females are dominant to any male. A baby Ring-tailed Lemur is born fully furred and able to move around. For the first few days it clings to its mother's belly *bottom right*, after which it is carried on her back.

Keeping in touch

Mammal mothers keep in touch with their babies very largely by smell. Every infant not only has its own distinctive smell, but when it suckles it also acquires some of the scent of its mother from the skin of her udder. Nest and pouch babies and those that cling to the mother must also share a common smell from their continuous close contact. Even a baby antelope or deer has some physical contact with its mother, since one of its main methods of communication is to vigorously prod its mother's flanks and udder with its muzzle before feeding. The mother frequently sniffs the baby to make sure it is her own. In a herd, of wildebeest for instance, each new calf is inspected and sniffed by all the mothers so that they can learn its scent. An African Elephant mother is able to keep in continuous close contact with her baby while the herd is on the move, sniffing it and fondling and guiding it with her trunk *left*.

Mammal mothers also talk to their babies and can probably instruct them by voice from a distance. The Topi is a large antelope abundant on the grassy plains of Africa. Females with young graze in small herds among zebras and wildebeest. The topi calves, when too young to graze with the adults, rest together in twos and threes, sometimes on a flat-topped termite mound. Each mother knows where her own baby is resting, and each baby is half-watching its own mother and picking up her scent all the time, even while dozing. When a female wants to suckle her calf she comes towards it, calling with a low bleat. Even when there are other calves nearby, only her own calf responds by getting up *top right* and running to her to begin suckling. The other calf does not even stir, but continues to wait calmly for its own mother *centre right*. Mammal babies also communicate with their mothers by voice, especially if in distress. Nest babies, such as those of the Greater Egyptian Gerbil *bottom right* emit squeaks so high-pitched they are higher than the human ear can detect. Ultrasonic squeaks from her babies have a very powerful effect on the mother gerbil, making her return at once to her nest to warm and comfort the brood, or move them to a safer nest if danger threatens.

Clinging Babies

The Grey Squirrel *left* is born in a bulky nest (called the drey) of twigs among treetop branches. There are usually three or four babies in a litter, born blind and naked. When very young they have a strong instinct to cling on tight, but they do not voluntarily leave the nest until capable of climbing well. The young Siamang *top right* is also born with a powerful instinct to cling at first to his mother's fur, later to branches and twigs. When old enough he progresses through the trees swinging along hand over hand – a form of locomotion known as brachiating. Bush Babies *bottom right* are tenacious clingers too and prodigious climbers and leapers. New-born babies cling at first to the mother's fur. Several mothers and their almost independent youngsters may crowd together by day in a hollow tree, coming out to bask in the evening sun before dispersing for the night to feed on insects.

Monkey Babies

Monkeys are continually on the move from one feeding place to another, performing all sorts of acrobatics in the normal course of food gathering. A mother monkey with a newborn baby is able to continue moving about quite freely and comfortably, using all four limbs, because she has a single baby and because the baby has a strong instinct to cling tight to her fur. Clinging for a baby monkey is as vital as breathing. It must not relax its grip for an instant, for its mother may take off in a violent leap in any direction and a baby that falls off is a dead baby. So a mother South American Spider Monkey *top right* can swing about unimpeded while her baby is quite secure, clinging to her fur.

The Yellow Baboon *left* is a big African monkey that feeds mainly on the ground. But a baboon infant must cling on just as tight to its mother's fur as must the baby of a more arboreal monkey, for baboons often climb trees or cliffs, and must sometimes run hard and make great leaps to escape danger. Naturally a new baby monkey claims the undivided attention of its mother. She herself becomes the centre of interest to all the other adult females who feel an intense desire to hold the new baby. At first its mother lets the aunties take it for very short spells, but only if the baby is happy; if it whimpers, she takes it back at once, and her right to do so, even from the bossiest female in the troop, is undisputed. The mother has very strong protective feelings towards her baby, as do all the other adult members of the troop. The baby's jerky, uncoordinated movement, its tiny size and its cries are part of its appeal, but its special colour also arouses strong emotions.

A baby Crab-eating Monkey of southeast Asia *bottom right* is born a different colour to its parents. It has a pink face, pink ears, and pink hands and feet which contrast with its black hair. This colour combination stirs strong feelings in the adult monkeys, ensuring that an infant receives intensive care from its mother while at the same time the adult males feel fiercely protective towards it.

Pick-a-back

At first, baby monkeys and apes cling beneath their mother's belly, so that when a Vervet Monkey *bottom left* walks along the ground, her baby peeps out upside down. At about three months old, it will begin to experiment with riding on her back, but when it first tries, it lacks the strength and dexterity to sit up, so clings across her, holding on with hands and feet. By about five months of age the baby will have mastered a more nonchalant jockey position, as has the young Olive Baboon *top left*. Ape babies are also carried in like manner for at least two years; in fact a baby Chimpanzee *right* may still be riding on its mother's back when it is four years old. By this time, the mother may well have another baby clinging to her breast, so she will encourage the older child to be less dependant on her.

Baby snatching

Just before the birth of her babies a female Arabian Spiny Mouse may become very broody and kidnap another mother's baby *top left*, carrying it about, grooming it, and even suckling it.

When mother mammals with helpless babies need to move them, they pick them up in the mouth. If not in a hurry, they pick them up gently across the shoulders, but if panicked by danger, grab them by the head or a leg, anything to remove the baby as fast as possible. When picked up the baby goes quite relaxed; if it struggled it would possibly get hurt, as well as making it more difficult for the mother to transport it to safety. Nest-making animals will move their babies to another nest if disturbed. The Red Fox vixen *bottom left* may have her cubs in one underground nest (known as an earth), then move them to another when they are a day or two old. New-born fox cubs look quite unlike their parents; they have short podgy muzzles, wrinkled brows and small turned down ears. Their eyes do not open until they are ten days or a fortnight old. At first their fur is dark chocolate-brown; gradually as they grow it turns to milk chocolate, but they do not start to grow red coats until they are about half-grown.

Lion cubs are born with their eyes partly open but they cannot see well for several weeks, and are quite helpless. For the first few months, they are left in some shady lair, when the mother goes off to hunt or get water. If she feels she must move them to a new nursery, she has to carry them one by one in her mouth *right*. At this age they are most vulnerable and may be killed by hyenas, wild dogs or eagles. It is for this reason that lionesses cooperate in rearing families, one staying on guard while the other is away. At about three months of age the cubs are allowed to go along with the lionesses on daily expeditions, although as soon as stalking begins in earnest the cubs must hide in the long grass. Lion cubs do not get their permanent teeth until they are a year old, so all this time they are dependant on their mother for food and protection.

Sleep

New-born babies spend nearly all their time deeply asleep. They, like us, have two kinds of sleep, light and deep sleep. During light sleep, the body makes frequent movements, but the brain is at rest. In deep sleep, only the eye and toe muscles twitch, whereas the brain is actively dreaming. So at first, a nestful of deep-sleeping babies lie hardly moving; but as they grow, they spend less time in deep sleep and more in light sleep. Then they twitch actively, making running movements.

When asleep, various changes take place in the way the body works. One of these is a faster growth rate. So it is chiefly while asleep that a baby animal such as a lion cub *below* does its growing. Adult horses spend little time asleep, mostly dozing as they stand. But a foal, such as the New Forest Pony *right* stretches out on the ground quite frequently to go into deep sleep. By the time a Hedgehog *left* is a month old, its sleep patterns will be the same as that of an adult.

Farm Babies

Domestic sheep usually give birth to a single lamb or twins. But with farming becoming more intensive, multiple births are being encouraged, with ewes producing three or four lambs at a time. The record number of lambs born to a domestic ewe is eight, but these all died. If a ewe loses her lambs, the shepherd tries to give her an orphan lamb or one from another ewe with twins or triplets. However, even a bereaved ewe is usually reluctant to accept a lamb that is not her own and will butt it away vigorously if it tries to suckle. She will have learnt the smell of her own lamb immediately after its birth, even if it was still-born. So the shepherd, in order to get the ewe to accept the strange baby skins her dead lamb and ties its fleece onto the foster-lamb to make it smell like the ewe's own. Often the ewe will then accept another's lamb and allow it to suckle, but not always. Sometimes the shepherd has to try other tricks, such as sprinkling a powerful scent over the foster-lamb to mask its own scent. In time the ewe learns and accepts the lamb's own scent, especially as it is also acquiring her scent as it suckles.

In the lowlands, lambs may be born very early in the year while it is still winter *top left*, but in the highlands it may be almost summer before the ewes begin lambing *bottom left*. In the highlands the cattle, too, are late calving *top right*, since winter is more prolonged in the north and at higher altitudes. As with every animal, it is to the species' as well as to the individual's advantage to produce its young when food is most abundant.

A domestic goat kid in a field of summer flowers has great charm and personality *bottom right*, and is most entertaining to watch as it skips about, surefooted, climbing on its reclining mother's back if there is nowhere else to climb. But the natural habitat of its wild ancestors is the barren hillside, and wherever domestic goats go they convert the landscape into their natural habitat. As a pet or producer of milk the goat is great; but let loose or allowed to multiply unchecked it is a maker of deserts. Goats will eat just about anything and in great quantity, so that they clear herbs and other low-growing vegetation. When there is little left for them to eat near the ground, they even climb into the trees to strip the leaves and twigs.

Piglets

Pigs were domesticated from the Wild Boar that still ranges right across Europe, North Africa and Asia. Wild Boars live mainly in woodlands, especially where there are mud holes in which they spend hours wallowing. Domestic pigs have not lost their ancestors' love of wallowing *top left.* Wild pigs will eat anything edible that they can find: acorns, beechmast, eggs, snails, carrion, mice, bark of trees, and roots of various kinds which they dig up with their tough snouts. Domestic pigs have not lost the ancestral rooting habit, either, and they are another animal capable of turning lush pasture into desert. For this reason domestic pigs are often restrained from rooting by having wire rings put through the nostrils. Pigs, wild or tame, cannot readily be herded; they are said to be too intelligent to go where they do not want to go. But they take well to living in sties. For this reason it is thought that the pig was not domesticated until man himself took to a settled life in houses.

Many of our modern pig breeds have lost the rangy shape and thick coat of coarse hair of the wild pig, and they have also lost the stripy pattern of the wild piglets *see the following page.* Many breeds today are white, which give us delightful pink piglets. Others are black and white, blotched or in a distinctive saddle-back pattern *centre and bottom left;* while others, such as the charming Vietnamese Pot-bellied Pig *top right* are all black. Under domestication, the sows produce twice as many piglets as do wild sows, and give birth several times a year, which is an economic asset to their owners.

The Warthog *bottom right* is the wild pig of the African grasslands. The sow's two to four piglets are usually born in a large burrow, probably excavated originally by an aardvark. The babies are reddish-brown at first, unstriped, and like all baby pigs are quite charming. The adult male Warthog, with his large warty face, straggly mane and huge curved tusks, has been called the most grotesque of all mammals, but even he has a distinctive charm. Females have shorter tusks than the boar, but even these can inflict nasty wounds in defence of the piglets.

Camouflaged Babies

The European Wild Boar roams the woods in family parties *left*. The stripy piglets, five to eight in a litter, are born in the spring. The sow makes a nest in which to farrow; she roots grass and plants into a heap in which she burrows to make a kind of tent and scrapes out the middle into a shallow bowl. The piglets make suckling movements as soon as they are born, and the sow nuzzles them to show them the teats. At about two weeks of age the sow leads her family from the nest, encouraging them with low grunts. If danger threatens, she gives a special warning call to the piglets, which immediately crouch down motionless, well camouflaged by their pale-striped coats.

The Brazilian Tapir *top right* is a big pig-like animal, related to the horse and the rhinoceros. It spends much of its time wallowing in water and mud, but is agile and can run swiftly when need be. The single young one is distinctively patterned with yellow and white longitudinal stripes and spots on the body and legs, but this pattern starts to disappear when it is about six months old.

The fawns of most species of deer such as the North American Mule Deer *centre* are dappled with white spots on a reddish ground for the first months of life. Although they are able to get on their feet and move about within hours of birth, fawns do not follow their mothers as do antelope calves. Instead, the mother leaves them among vegetation where they 'freeze' motionless if danger threatens, their spotted coats helping to conceal them in the dappled light and shade. For this reason, people who chance upon a very young Roe kid lying apparently alone in the woods *bottom right* rush to the conclusion that it has been abandoned by its mother. Nothing could be further from the truth, for the anxious doe is surely watching from a distance, and if the kid is not taken she will return to lead it to another bed and suckle it. Fawns are very delicate, nervous creatures and should always be left to their own mother to rear, unless it is known for certain that she has been killed or injured.

Zoo Babies

The zoo used to be regarded as just a place of entertainment for children, but today it is much more than that: it certainly provides attractive exhibits, but also does research into the needs of captive animals, provides educational programmes for schools, and conserves fast-disappearing wild populations by breeding. Some species now breed readily in zoos, once their physical and psychological needs have been catered for. Years ago, when lions were kept behind bars in tiny cells, they did not breed. Today, an appealing spotted cub *top left* is no longer the great rarity it once was. The Giraffe, from the bush-lands of Africa, which produces the tallest baby in the animal kingdom *right,* also breeds well in captivity if given the right conditions; while the Scimitar Oryx *bottom left,* an endangered species, is probably doing better in safari parks than it is in its native Sahara Desert.

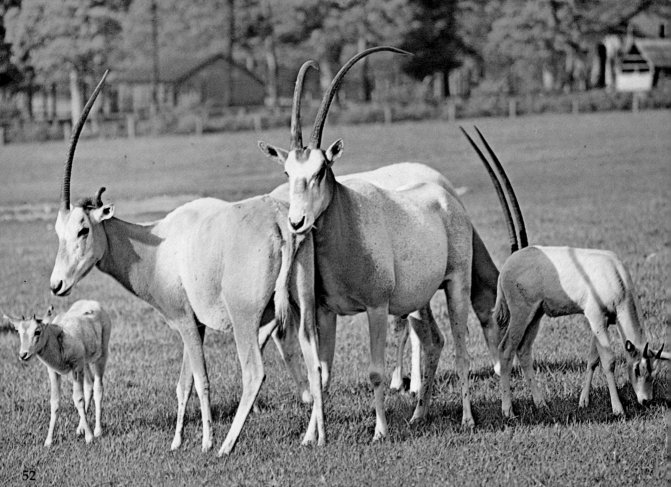

Play

The importance of play to a baby animal can hardly be exaggerated. In social animals such as monkeys, infants of the same age group learn how to get along with their fellows. A baby monkey reared in a cage alone with its mother and therefore deprived of play with other monkeys is unable later to establish social relationships within a troop, and is even incapable of mating when it grows up. When introduced to other young monkeys it appears completely terrified of them, and never learns how to get along with them. On the other hand, a baby monkey reared by a human foster-mother but allowed to play with other monkey babies, learns in their rough-and-tumble games how to become an effective member of monkey society. The mother is of prime importance to a very young baby, for without her he could not survive; but as he grows, his playmates are of equal importance if he is to grow up well adjusted.

Among less social animals play is still of great importance. Young Polar Bears *top right* wrestle and chase one another, play follow-my-leader as they race over rocks and ice, then leap into the sea and swim in tandem. Often unusual weather conditions will result in even more exuberant scampering around: many animals encountering snow for the first time go wild in it, like the Donkey foal *centre*. In Africa a rainstorm may be the trigger that sends normally staid animals such as the solemn wildebeest scampering and bucking like calves, while elephants trample about pushing over trees apparently just for the fun of it. Water, whether falling or settled, is always good to play in: Indian Elephants love to wallow and spray themselves *left*, showing their obvious enjoyment; while a Crab-eating Macaque will just 'monkey about' in the water, not only leaping into it and swimming, but also quite seriously experimenting with it *bottom right*. All this is more than the natural exuberance of youth. Such energetic play builds up muscles, develops agility and judgment, and rehearses hunting techniques. It also helps animals to react with that extra speed and precision in an emergency which can mean the difference between survival or death.

55

Grooming

Apes and monkeys spend a great deal of time grooming one another, a comforting habit which helps strengthen bonds between individuals. Mothers groom their infants frequently. A mother Chimpanzee *top left* will go through her child's fur picking out any foreign particles such as dirt, ticks, burrs or dried skin, and can even extract splinters with her fingers or lips, or delicately remove a speck of grit from an eye. Other social animals groom each other, sometimes as part of courtship; and even youngsters like these two Przewalski's Wild Horses *bottom left* nibble away at each other's withers in a mutual grooming session. Grooming is important in keeping fur and skin clean, but it also has other benefits. When a Rabbit grooms its ears it licks oil from them off its paws *right*. This oil contains vitamin D which is produced in sunlight; if a growing rabbit is kept in the shade or prevented from washing its ears, it may develop rickets.

Underground Babies

Many animals that give birth to helpless babies hide them away in underground burrows for safety until the young are old enough to make their own way to the surface. Red Fox cubs are born in an earth at about the end of March or beginning of April, and they will remain underground for the first month of their lives. Often it is four weeks to the day when the first adventurous chocolate-coloured cub creeps cautiously from the entrance to the earth on an exploratory expedition *top left*. Although its eyes have already been open for half its life, they are still a short-sighted baby blue-grey, and it cannot see a great deal. Its food will be brought to it at the entrance to the earth by the vixen, and also by the dog-fox which takes an active part in rearing his family, although he usually gives the food to the vixen who then gives it to the cubs. Badger cubs also remain in their underground sett for their first month, but then, like the fox cubs, they begin to explore farther afield, learning to find food for themselves *right*. Water Vole babies are born in a grass nest at the end of a tunnel, usually above water level, in a bank close to a river or stream. When they emerge they do not need to be instructed in food-finding techniques: their food, the grass, grows all around them *centre left*. Other small rodents make their nest in underground burrows to escape extremes of cold, heat or both. The Small Naked-soled Gerbil *bottom left* lives in the semi-deserts of East Africa, where the days are very hot under a blazing sun. The burrow is not only cool, it is also moist, so underground the tiny animals are able to stay at a comfortable temperature without losing precious moisture from their bodies. After the sun has gone down and the air temperature has dropped, the mother and her young can come out to forage for seeds which provide them with both food and moisture in a land where drinking water is mostly non-existent.

Growing up

The most dangerous time of life for nest-babies is when they first venture from the safety of the burrow or den and begin to look after themselves. Not only have they to learn their way around and where to find food, they are also quite inexperienced in coping with dangers. Luckily, they learn fast. Within days, young Common Rats have learned to skip along the trails of other rats and find food scraps thrown out by wasteful humans *left*. The young Raccoon forages in a swamp *top right* finding all kinds of edibles such as worms, frogs, birds' eggs, crayfish or berries. The ability to enjoy such a wide variety of food is the secret of the Raccoon's success. The Hedgehog *bottom right* also enjoys a similarly wide range of such delicacies as his nose leads him to, while his prickly back gives him an instant defence from all but the strongest predators.

Independence

As a baby animal grows it acquires the strength and skills it needs to look after itself. As self-assurance builds up so its dependence on its mother decreases until finally it is ready to care for itself. However, many youngsters remain with their parents for some time longer, being reluctant to set out into the unknown on their own. Often the parents have to chase the youngsters away. This is hard, but necessary, and the chief reason for it in many species is lack of space. Fox cubs, for instance, approaching adult size, cause physical overcrowding in the nursery earth; and the territory over which the parent foxes hunt can support only a certain number of adults, if the food supply is not to be dangerously reduced. So the cubs are forced to move out and find their own dens and territories. Some young animals such as raccoons have an inherent urge to wander off on their own anyway, so merely drift away without being chased out. In other species such as squirrels and mice it is the parent that leaves home, the mother deserting her almost-grown young to dig a new nursery for her next litter.

The length of time any young animal stays with its mother varies greatly, depending on how quickly the baby matures and also on the breeding cycle of the female. Small rodents that give birth to litters every few weeks in the summer, turn their rapidly-maturing babies out or desert them when they are only three to four weeks old. In contrast, a donkey foal, if it were in the wild *right* might stay with its mother until the following spring when her next foal is born. A Brown Bear cub *left* usually stays with its mother for over a year, denning up with her for the winter, or in its own den a few yards from hers. Great ape children mature most slowly and are therefore cared for longest of any animal, and stay in the family group for five years or more, even when younger siblings are born. But human young mature slowest of all, and stay within the family group at least twice as long as any animal children.

INDEX

CLB 1053
This edition published 1987 by Colour Library
Books, Ltd.
86 Epsom Road, Guildford, Surrey, England.
© Text: Jane Burton
© Illustrations: Jane Burton/Bruce Coleman Ltd.
Printed and bound in Spain by Cronion S.A.
ISBN: 0-904681-15-7